Sports Illustrated KIDS

# STARS OF SPORTS

# COCO GAUFF

## TENNIS CHAMPION

by Matt Chandler

CAPSTONE PRESS
a capstone imprint

Stars of Sports is published by Capstone Press, an imprint of Capstone.
1710 Roe Crest Drive, North Mankato, Minnesota 56003
www.capstonepub.com

SPORTS ILLUSRATED KIDS is a trademark of ABG-SI LLC. Used with permission.

**Library of Congress Cataloging-in-Publication Data is available on the Library of Congress website.**
ISBN: 978-1-4966-9524-6 (library binding)
ISBN: 978-1-9771-5403-3 (eBook PDF)

**Editorial Credits**
Mandy Robbins, editor; Elyse White and Lori Bye, designers; Eric Gohl, media researcher; Spencer Rosio, production specialist

**Photo Credits**
Dreamstime: Featureflash, 26; Getty Images: BARBARA GINDL, 16, 17, BEN STANSALL, 19, Cameron Spencer, 10, Icon Sportswire, 5, Matthew Stockman, 14, 15, Phil Harris/Mirrorpix, 21, TPN, 9, Visionhaus, 18, Wayne Taylor, 13; Newscom: Abaca Press/Dubreuil Corinne/Abaca/Sipa USA, 11, Dubreuil Corinne/Sipa USA, 7, Jeff Romance/ZUMA Press, 28, John Angelillo/UPI, 23, Mike Egerton/ZUMA Press, 25, Phil Harris/Mirrorpix, 20, ZUMA Press/Jeff Romance, Cover; Shutterstock: kireewong foto, 1; Sports Illustrated: Erick W. Rasco, 27

Copyright ABG-SI LLC. Used under license.

**Direct Quotations**
Page 6, from Aug. 29, 2019, *Good Morning America* article, "15-year-old tennis star Coco Gauff says she hopes 'to be the greatest of all time,'" goodmorningamerica.com
Page 12, from Feb. 20, 2020, WTA article, "Corey Gauff named PTR Touring Coach of the Year," wtatennis.com
Page 19, line 4, from July 2, 2019, CNN article, "15-year-old Cori 'Coco' Gauff stuns Venus Williams at Wimbledon," cnn.com
Page 19, line 9, from Jan. 20, 2020, *The New York Times* article, "Coco Gauff Vaults from Obscurity to Stardom, but the Result Is the Same," nytimes.com
Page 20, from July 5, 2019, Reuters article, "Wimbledon crowd go loco for Coco as dream continues," uk.reuters.com
Page 22, from Jan. 20, 2020, *Yahoo! Money* article, "Teen Tennis Phenom Coco Gauff Defeats Venus Williams Once Again at Australian Open," money.yahoo.com
Page 22 sidebar, from Oct. 16, 2019, *Guardian* article, "Coco Gauff: 'My generation has just decided it's time to speak up,'" theguardian.com
Page 23, from Aug. 21, 2019, *Teen Vogue* article, "Cori 'Coco' Gauff on Winning, Fame, and Life Off the Tennis Court," teenvogue.com
Page 26, from undated *Behind the Racquet* story, "Coco Gauff," behindtheracquet.com

All internet sites appearing in back matter were available and accurate when this book was sent to press.

# TABLE OF CONTENTS

Glossary terms are **BOLD** on first use.

# JUNIOR CHAMPION!

It looked like the end of an amazing run for rising tennis star Cori "Coco" Gauff. The 14-year-old had made it to the finals of the 2018 girls' division of the French Open. She had a chance to win her first tennis **major**.

Then it all seemed to fall apart. Early on, Gauff trailed against fellow American Caty McNally. She lost the first set. But Gauff never gave up. She fought back and won the second set against 17-year-old McNally. It set up a showdown for the title.

## FACT

Tennis is divided into games, sets, and matches. A player wins a single game. A set goes to the first player to win six games. A match is the best of three sets in women's tennis.

⟨⟨⟨ Gauff brought her best game to the 2018 French Open.

It took 13 games to settle it. One of the biggest moments was when Gauff won a 17-**volley** serve. McNally delivered a shot just over the net. Gauff raced to the net, stretched, and returned the shot. It was a perfect shot to win the point. Gauff had won her first tennis major!

Coco Gauff was born on March 13, 2004, in Delray Beach, Florida. She has two brothers, Cody and Cameron. Their mom, Candi, was a teacher and a track-and-field champion. Their dad, Corey, worked in health care. He played tennis as a boy. Later on, he played college basketball at Division I Georgia State University.

Both of Gauff's parents wanted their children to follow in their footsteps and play sports. Gauff grew up playing tennis, soccer, and gymnastics. When she was just four, the family was watching tennis player Serena Williams compete on television. Her dad told Gauff that Williams was "the G.O.A.T.," meaning the greatest of all time. Gauff immediately said, "Daddy, I want to be the G.O.A.T.!" That's still her goal today.

<<< Gauff's parents at her side during the 2017 U.S. Open

# TRAINING IN FLORIDA

Gauff was six years old when she remembers picking up a racket for the first time.

By the time she was seven, her parents thought her talent and passion meant she had a real future in the sport. But they had moved to Atlanta, Georgia, and didn't think it was the best place to train. They moved back to Florida, where many of the best tennis training centers were. Her dad became her coach, and her mom began **homeschooling** her. That way Gauff could focus on tennis.

Gauff quickly became a force in junior tennis. In 2012, she won the Little Mo, a tournament for tennis players who are under eight years old. Two years later, she won the United States Tennis Association (USTA) Clay Court National 12-under title. At age 10, she was the youngest champion in the tournament's history.

⟨⟨⟨ Gauff and her father, Corey, after practicing for the 2019 U.S. Open

After her Clay Court title, people paid attention to Gauff. Tennis experts called her a future superstar. Coaches, fans, and other players called her a natural or a **prodigy**. But Gauff's father said it was hard work that made his daughter a top **prospect** at only 12 years old.

⟨⟨⟨ Gauff plays her first junior round at the 2018 Wimbledon Championships.

Junior tennis is divided into different levels. Gauff was a leader at each level she played. Her biggest win may have been the junior title at the French Open in 2018. But she also made it to the quarterfinals at Wimbledon as a junior in 2018. Those big wins helped earn her the spot as the top-ranked junior player in the world.

# COACH DAD

Gauff's dad, Corey, was a great basketball player. But he hadn't played competitive tennis since he was a kid. He had never taught tennis, but that didn't stop him from deciding to coach his daughter. He wanted to be the one to guide her as she trained to be a pro. He wanted to follow the direction of Richard Williams, the father of Venus and Serena Williams. He coached his famous daughters to become two of the most successful players of all time.

Corey also works with other coaches who help his daughter develop her game. His coaching includes a lot of positive encouragement.

"He gave me the best advice," Gauff said after one tournament. "I guess he didn't really tell me how to play—just to stay calm and stay focused . . ."

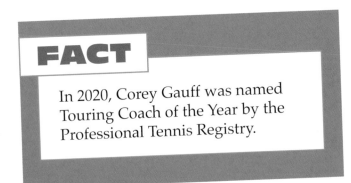

**FACT**

In 2020, Corey Gauff was named Touring Coach of the Year by the Professional Tennis Registry.

Corey Gauff advises Coco during the 2020 Australian Open.

# CHAPTER THREE
# MAKING IT BIG!

By 2019, Gauff was a star on the Women's Tennis Association (WTA) tour. Fans mobbed her for autographs and photos. Her matches drew some of the biggest crowds.

⟨⟨⟨ Gauff at the 2019 Miami Open

Gauff delivers a backhand return during the 2019 Miami Open.

Gauff's fame is still new. She played her first WTA event in early 2019. She earned a **wild-card** entry into the Miami Open. Her dad wasn't sure she should play. At 15 years old, he didn't know if his daughter was ready. Boy was he wrong!

Gauff was matched up against her former singles opponent and doubles partner, Caty McNally. In the biggest match of her young career, Gauff lost the opening set, 6–3. Then the teen took over, winning the next two sets 6–3 and 6–4. Though she was swept in the second round by Russian Daria Kasatkina, Gauff proved she belonged on the WTA Tour!

# WTA CHAMPION!

After just seven months on tour, Gauff entered the 2019 Upper Austria Ladies Linz event. The teen had to beat four players to earn a spot in the finals—and she did it!

She faced former French Open champ Jeļena Ostapenko, who was seven years her senior. The women split the first two sets of the match, 1–1.

⟨⟨⟨ Gauff serves to her opponent at the 2019 Upper Austria Ladies Linz event.

In the final set, Gauff brought her best game.
She took a 5–0 lead. Gauff looked unstoppable.
Ostapenko battled back to win two games, but it
wasn't enough. In the final game, Gauff was one point
from winning the match. Ostapenko returned a volley
long. It took a video review to award the point and
the championship to Gauff. She had won her first
professional singles title!

# CHAPTER FOUR
# AMONG LEGENDS

In 2019, Gauff was a surprise qualifier for the **main draw** at Wimbledon. The 15-year-old found herself across the court from five-time Wimbledon champion Venus Williams.

⟨⟨⟨ Gauff concentrates on returning a shot to Venus Williams.

⟨⟨⟨ Venus Williams congratulates Gauff after the teenager beat her at Wimbledon.

Williams was expected to easily beat the teen. Instead, Gauff swept her in two straight sets, 6–4, 6–4.

Gauff recalled what she said to Williams after the upset win. "I just told her I wouldn't be here if it wasn't for her, she's so inspiring."

Gauff faced Williams in a rematch in the first round of the Australian Open in 2020. Gauff beat her for the second straight time, 7–6, 6–3.

After the win, Gauff described the feeling. "My mission is to be the greatest," she said. "But for today, my mission was to win. I didn't want to let the nerves come to me."

# NEWFOUND FAME

Gauff's third-round match at Wimbledon had to be moved to Centre Court to allow more fans to watch. Gauff talked in interviews about what that instant fame was like.

"I remember before I played Venus, as you know, when you walk to leave the practice courts, there are people waiting. One little kid asked me for a picture. Then after the next day, after I played Venus, everybody was screaming my name."

⟨⟨⟨ Gauff faced off against Polona Hercog in the third round at Wimbledon in 2019.

Gauff faced former number-one ranked Simona Halep in Round 16. Gauff was the new fan favorite to win, but Halep was too strong. She easily defeated Gauff. Still, Gauff had beaten long odds. The teenager who had played her first WTA match only four months earlier had reached the fourth round of the biggest tournament in tennis!

⟨⟨⟨ Gauff returns a shot to Polona Hercog in the third round at Wimbledon in 2019.

# THE PRICE OF FAME

When Gauff went to Wimbledon in 2019, she had 30,000 Instagram followers. When she came home, she had 300,000! Her new fame came with a lot of new pressure for the teenager.

*"When I was younger, I was just dreaming about winning tournaments and winning slams I guess, and I didn't think about all that would come with it,"* she said.

## Social Media Star

Gauff is a social-media superstar. She has more than one million followers. Social media let athletes connect directly with fans. That can be a great thing. But it can also give mean people easy access. After her first pro win, social media blew up with people attacking Gauff. She refused to let it bother her. "I just used it as motivation to prove them wrong," she said.

Despite the fame, Gauff still finds time for most things a typical teenager enjoys. She hangs out with her friends, loves TikTok, hip-hop music, and watching *Dancing with the Stars*.

In the middle of her newfound fame and success, Gauff tries to keep a level head.

"I try not to think about it, because it'll put too much pressure on [me]," she says.

⟨⟨⟨ Gauff takes a selfie with a young fan.

# BECOMING THE BEST

It's no secret that Gauff wants to be the greatest. That begins with earning the number-one WTA ranking. By early 2020, Gauff had broken the top 50. It was impressive for a 16-year-old player so new to the tour.

Gauff still has a long way to go. She had competed well in WTA tournaments in Miami and Austria, and her Wimbledon showing had been impressive. But in March of 2020, the world faced the coronavirus **pandemic**. Sporting events all over the world were canceled or postponed. Professional tennis was no exception.

Could Gauff have increased her ranking even more throughout the 2020 season? Might she have made an impressive showing at Wimbledon again? The world will never know. But she continues to work hard and train. When professional tennis tournaments resume, Gauff will be ready.

**FACT**

Gauff is represented by Team8, the sports marketing company cofounded by tennis legend Roger Federer.

‹‹‹ Gauff gets some air while returning a shot during the third round of Wimbledon in 2019.

## CHAPTER FIVE
# A BRIGHT FUTURE

At 16 years old, Gauff's future seemed bright. She was on track to become the number-one player in the world. But in 2020, she wrote an article about feeling depressed. She felt alone. The pressure was becoming too much. She talked about wanting to quit tennis.

<<< Gauff poses on the red carpet at the 2019 E! People's Choice Awards.

*"I just found myself not enjoying what I loved,"* she said in the article. *"I realized I needed to start playing for myself and not other people."*

Since then, the teen says she has felt better about the pressure of the game. She has embraced her new position as a role model for young girls. And, most importantly, she says she still loves playing tennis.

## Making Money off the Court

By 2020, Gauff had collected more than $800,000
in winnings on the tennis court. That may sound
like a lot, but it's nothing compared to what she
can earn off the court. Successful athletes such as
Gauff sign endorsement contracts. That means they
team up with companies to promote their products.
Gauff earned $1 million in 2019 alone from her
endorsement deals.

# LOOKING AHEAD

Gauff is still a teen. She is a promising tennis player, but will it last? The pressure on young players can be tough. Fans, coaches, and sponsors all push them to win. The practice and travel can be hard. The injuries can add up. But Gauff could also continue to grow and develop her game. Most experts believe she has the chance to be the top women's player in the world. Time will tell if Coco Gauff will become one of the greatest to ever play the game.

⟨⟨⟨ Gauff waves at the crowd after a 2020 match at the University of Miami.

# TIMELINE

**2004**   Gauff is born in Delray Beach, Florida, on March 13.

**2012**   Gauff captures the "Little Mo" 8-Under national title.

**2016**   Gauff joins the International Tennis Federation Junior Circuit tour.

**2017**   As a 12-year-old, Gauff advances to the semifinals in the Les Petits As–Le Mondial Lacoste.

**2018**   She wins the girls' division at the French Open.

**2018**   Gauff makes her debut as a professional on the ITF Women's Circuit, winning her first match.

**2018**   Gauff signs a major endorsement deal with New Balance.

**2019**   Gauff plays her first match on the WTA tour, at the Miami Open in March.

**2019**   Gauff wins her first WTA singles title, the Upper Austria Ladies Linz, in October.

**2019**   Gauff defeats Venus Williams at Wimbledon.

# GLOSSARY

**ENDORSEMENT** (in-DORS-muhnt)—the act of an athlete wearing, promoting, or using a product, often for money

**HOMESCHOOL** (HOME-skool)—when parents teach their children school subjects from home

**MAIN DRAW** (MAYN DRAW)—the part of a tournament that matches up the final players competing

**MAJOR** (MAY-jur)—in tennis, the four biggest tournaments of the year; they are the U.S. Open, the French Open, the Australian Open, and Wimbledon

**PANDEMIC** (pan-DEM-ik)—a disease that spreads over the entire world and affects many people

**PRODIGY** (PRAH-duh-jee)—someone who, at a young age, is extraordinarily good at an activity

**PROSPECT** (PROSS-pekt)—a player who is just starting out, but experts believe has a chance to make it to the professional level of his or her sport

**VOLLEY** (VOL-ee)—a series of hits between opponents back and forth over the net

# READ MORE

Cline-Ransome, Lesa. *Game Changers: The Story of Venus and Serena Williams.* New York: Simon & Schuster Books for Young Readers, 2018.

Hellebuyck, Adam, and Laura Deimel. *Tennis Grand Slam.* Ann Arbor, MI: Cherry Lake Publishing, 2020.

Scheff, Matt. *Naomi Osaka: Tennis Star.* Lake Elmo, MN: Focus Readers, 2020.

# INTERNET SITES

*Women's Tennis Association*
wtatennis.com

*ESPN Player Profile, Cori Gauff*
espn.com/tennis/player/_/id/3626/cori-gauff

*United States Tennis Association*
usta.com/en/home.html

# INDEX